The Ronald
My Love

By Cathy Burnham Martin

The Ronald
Daydreams, Wonderments & Other Ponderings

By Cathy Burnham Martin

Quiet Thunder Publishing

ISBN 978-1-939220-15-8 Paperback
ISBN 978-1-939220-16-5 eBook
Library of Congress Control Number 2014957195
Manchester, NH USA
©2014

All poetry, prose, and photographs by
Cathy Burnham Martin and friends
with thanks to God for our
blessings and bounty

www.GoodLiving123.com

This collection of *Daydreams, Wonderments, and Other Ponderings* was lovingly assembled for Ron by Cathy Burnham Martin,
the baby...
who became
your Baby.

**Before you, my world seemed a whirlwind of family and arts, career and community.
It appeared larger than Life at times...**

Cathy clockwise from top right: Van Johnson; after winning Miss New Hampshire 1975 title; Robert Guillaume & John Sununu; Robert Wagner; Carole King; Arlo Guthrie; Roy Orbison

But you were out there...
struggling to be loved...
searching for hope.

Ron during our first
trip to Aruba

We're all scared of hurting,
of love deserting
   us once again

We run and hide from emotion.
And with devotion
   we pretend

We're happy to be solo and free!
No one can see
   we're on the mend.

That emptiness inside we feel –
"Alone" is so real.
   Remember when….

Ogunquit Beach, Maine in January

While we hope to be held and long to be wanted,
We devote much strength to our defenses.

We learn to deny any feelings inside,
Living instead with cool, but shallow pretenses.

For sadness to end...
We must accept ourselves for who
we are and who we can be.
With time, the bars of pain will
soften and release us to be free.

Just as flowers bend...
Though hard rains fall, and wind cuts
like a knife,
We too can learn to love the
sunshine, which brings back life.

And then we fly...
Because we know we have finally
learned how to live,
And we receive even more than the
plenty we give.

So, let us try...
To simply treasure each precious day
as it arrives
So we can capture the peace that can
rule humble lives.

Then you waltz in... grinning that grin!

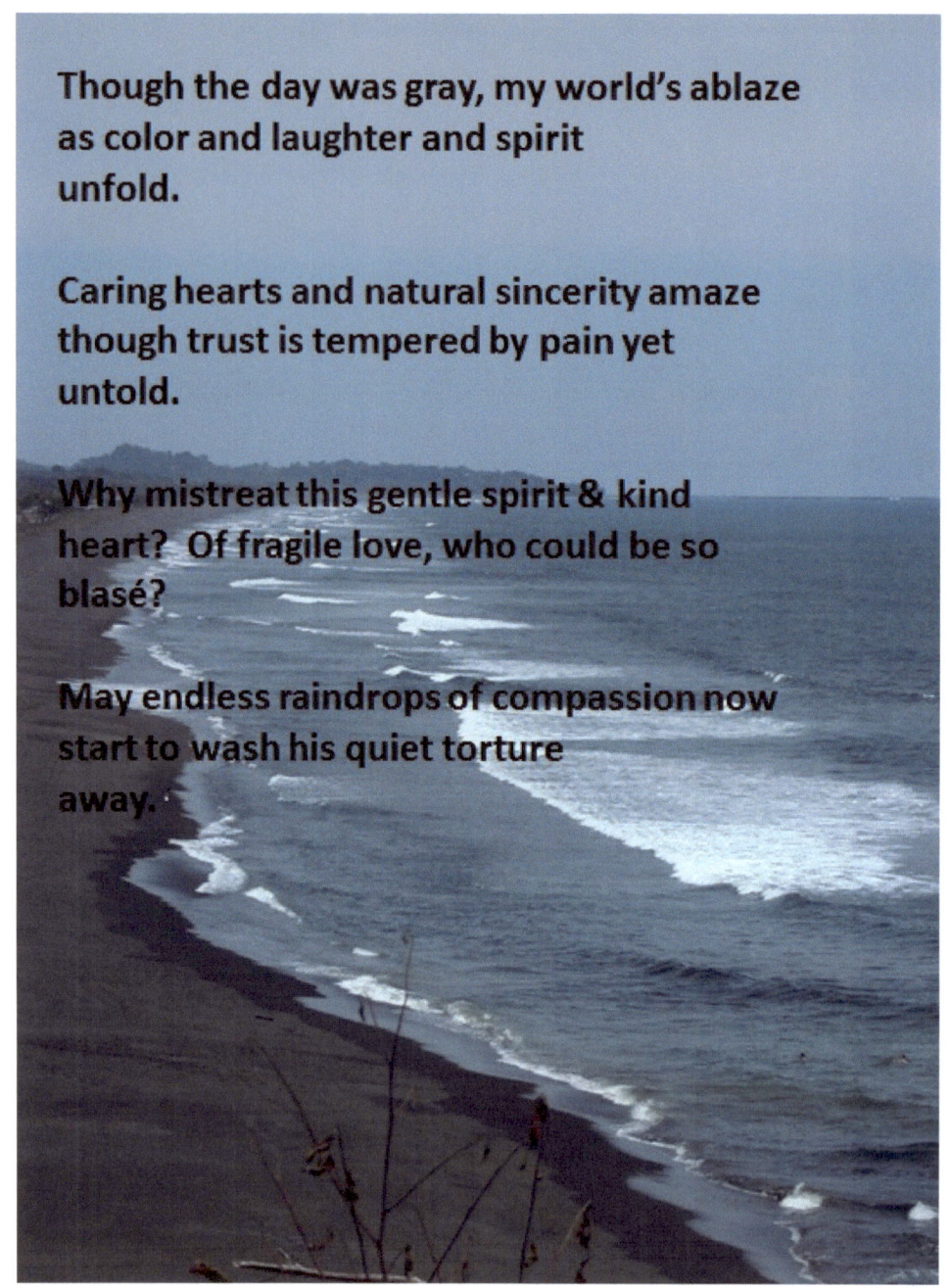

Though the day was gray, my world's ablaze
as color and laughter and spirit
unfold.

Caring hearts and natural sincerity amaze
though trust is tempered by pain yet
untold.

Why mistreat this gentle spirit & kind
heart? Of fragile love, who could be so
blasé?

May endless raindrops of compassion now
start to wash his quiet torture
away.

First your wit, smile, laughter and conversation
Capturing my imagination and stirring my heart.

Then your kiss, so playfully soft and sweet
With your gentle touch melting all chance of retreat.

As though to become part of each other, we hug so tightly;
Long-forgotten passion rises, rippling through me, ever so lightly.

Your hands mold me like clay, as you take control.
I'm yours; you capture my mind, body, and soul.

Aboard Princess cruise in Caribbean

Arriving at Easter Seals event & meeting our escort, Brandon

You joined in some of my volunteer endeavors... and even had some fun.

Cooking for the Kids at Kiwanis "Fish with a Child" event

Sometimes I took you places that excited you... like the new Yankee Stadium during an Easter Seals New York Gala.

Usually, it was *you*... whisking *me* off to exotic places... like this trip to Puerto Rico! Lots of memories... lots of sharing. Thank you for it all, my Love.

Ron & Cathy at The Baths, Virgin Gorda, British Virgin Islands

Mall in Milan, Italy

Menaggio,

on the shore of

Lake Como

in the Italian Alps

Gondolas in Venice, Italy

Swimming in the world's largest underground river; Cozumel, Mexico

West End, Roatan, Honduras

The most amazing ruins in the Mediterranean area... in Ephesus, Turkey

Those round, soulful eyes
    and your big, loving heart
Reveal who you really are
    and have been from the start:

A wonderful man filled with truth,
        filled with love...
The answer to prayers
    straight from God above.

Christ the Redeemer atop Corcovado in Rio de Janeiro, Brazil

Cathy on our balcony overlooking Copacabana and Ipanema Beaches, Rio de Janeiro, Brazil

At the Trump National Doral Miami in Doral, Florida

Ron dancing with a dolphin in Anguilla

I just think about your

warm eyes and smiling face,

and I start smiling all over!

Blue Grotto,
Isle of Capri, Italy

During our romantic island tour
for two…

a boat, a captain, a bottle of wine
and a chunk of cheese and bread
for two lovers.

Cathy snapping photo of Jeremy & Bevy at the Acropolis in Athens, Greece

View from Bon Appetit in Dunedin, Florida

You captured my heart

and breathed life back

into every dusty corner of my soul.

For he is thoughtful and witty, gentle and kind, and through his eyes I see his soul dance.

His fingertips spark passions, as do his words in my mind; his smile engulfs all doubt that I should take this chance.

What music is to love
this man is to passion:

A patiently sizzling progression to melt
The most defiant ice fortress I fashion,

An all-consuming melody
of soft and gentle fascination,

With a firmly undeniable harmony that defies imagination!

You say that you would have found me anywhere...
no matter what, no matter where.
I'm glad you were led to New Hampshire, and we
started to share.

Cathy's Mom, Dad and Aunt Phyllis are just behind us.

Loving you is
>   an amazing sensation
Because you are
>   such a rare combination.

It matters not what's in vogue
>   or considered "fashion."
You have values
>   powered by passion.

The fact that you're smart
>   and remarkably funny
Just makes me more glad
>   that you are my Honey.

I've got the old feeling still in my heart!

After the fall, Cathy starting down Sliding Rock in Brazilian rain forest, inland from Parati

We've had our foibles and faux pas...

and loved each other through them all.

Burn, Baby, Burn...
Mill Spring, North Carolina...
one of the many fires that did
NOT need a 911 call.

Food remains a shared enjoyment, both dining out & cooking in. And, okay... thankfully you do not typically choose to consume "brain-sized" burritos like this one in Columbus, North Carolina. It surely made us laugh!

Ron carving up rib-eye steaks for the grill

Ron & Dr. Jeremy Moody making pizzas at the Lawn Club Grill on the top deck of the Celebrity Silhouette

Food in exotic places from lunch at Palmeras in Palestine to game grilled at Las Nazarenas in Buenos Aires to fish from Yardenit on the River Jordan

Lunch with Dr. J & Bevy near the Spanish Steps in Rome, Italy

Enjoying one of many lovely dinners, while cruising the Mediterranean with Dr. Jeremy and Beverly Reed Moody

Loving great food, we have dined in wonderful places from Bern's Steakhouse in Tampa, Florida to virtually everywhere in New Hampshire, including Cotton, where we celebrated many anniversaries of our first date.

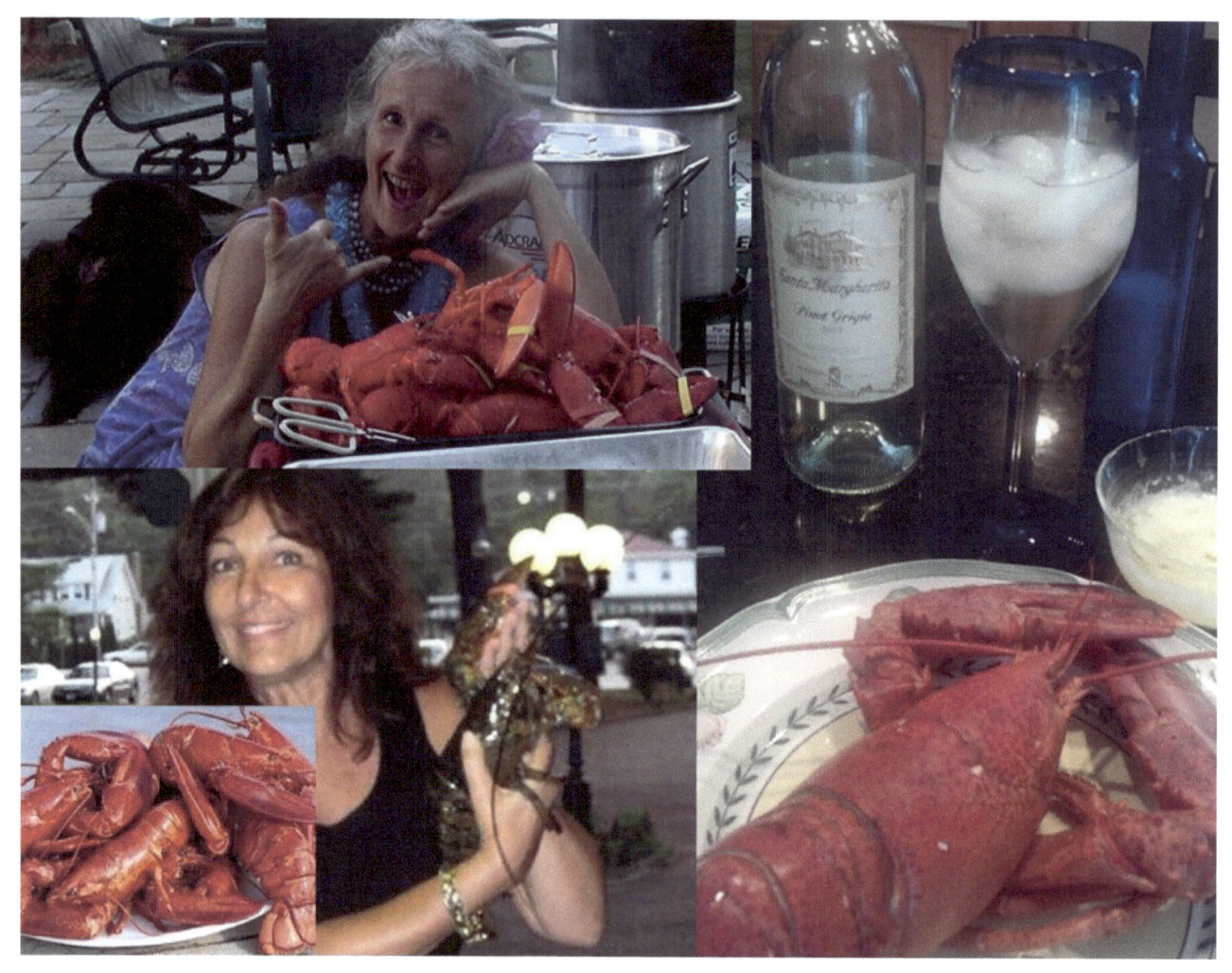

Oh, and did I mention my passion for lobster?

So many great times are even better because we share a great wealth of good friends!

Celebrating Paul's birthday at Angelina's in Concord, New Hampshire 2012. Left to Right: Ron & Cathy Martin, Steve & Kathie Burnell, Dottie & Paul Sullivan

Happy New Year

at the

Hanover Street Chop House

Ron & Cathy with Nancy Keller & Allen Von der Hoff; Al Marracco with Bandit & Baci; Ron & Cathy with Eric Mostrom in Greenville, SC

Friends

**make all the difference in the world...
every day.**

Ben Gamache with Ron; Deb & Bob Briggs in SC; Ley & Steve Brooks, Ron, Al & Peg Marracco, & Cathy at Shibley's in Alton Bay, NH

We are bountifully blessed with so many wonderful friends.

Ben Gamache and Cathy at Newport, Rhode Island boat show

Bevy Dahhhling, Dr. J,

Lady Catherine & Sir Ronald

at a sidewalk café in

Montreal, Canada

Al & Peg Marracco, Steve & Ley Brooks, Ron with Alden Moore

Clockwise from top right:
Steve & Kathie Burnell,
Allen von der Hoff & Nancy Keller,
Kevin & Christine Pederson,
Patte & Jim Powers

Left: Jim Lurvey & Janice Gilbert in Marco Island
Right: Enjoying Hollywood Beach, Florida with Katie Karl and Bob Lajoie

With Mitt Romney at his Wolfeboro, New Hampshire home; 2005

Hmmm... a few exotic buddies along the way...

like Ron's iguanas

in Costa Rica

Giraffes at the zoo in Barcelona, Spain

...and our buddies at home

Jeeter purrs, Take me!"
Bandit adds, "Tell me you
can resist <u>this</u> face!"

Crisp autumn leaves
Cracking as they spin –
Locking our gaze
As they dance in the wind...

Grotesquely cackling
Like the lies we get told
Withering and fading
The dreams we were sold.

We've worked hard through many seasons and transformed our house into a loving and lovely home.

Doing chores with each other makes any job more fun!

Things go right. Things go wrong.
Just try to remember you are not alone...

I am here to help in all ways I can.
I've told you before, and I'll tell you again:
All the toys... the "stuff"... cars and houses just flatter.
Only YOU, Sir Ronald, only *you* matter.

Left: 2011 Halloween Snow

Right: 2013 pre-Christmas snowfall in Goffstown, New Hampshire

Captain Ron... enjoying his hard-earned escape to Lake Winnipesaukee

Lake Winnipesaukee, Gilford, New Hampshire

You set my heart free,

then rightfully claimed it

as your own.

Sunset at Mountainview Yacht Club,
Gilford, New Hampshire

Wake from "Miss Behavin' Too" on Lake Winnipesaukee

Bandit & Cathy lounging on Lake Winnipesaukee, New Hampshire

Bandit rules both in and out of the water!

Sky Blue Pink & a Duck Cloud

The colors rise in full harmony now blinding the sky's gray.

And with his kiss my heart again is young.

I don't know how, but he is here, and I want him to stay...

this unfulfilled maestro with a song to be sung.

2013 Bike Week,
Weirs Beach,
New Hampshire

When stress
Wears you
D
O
W
N

Remember...
I'm right here
To pump you
UP

2013 sun setting on Lake Winnipesaukee, as we listened to "Colour of the Sun" during Jimmy Buffett's debut of his new CD, "Songs from St. Somewhere" on Radio Margaritaville

Whether Hope is alive in your heart or struggling to survive,
I am still right here...
just as I always will be...
holding your hand when you need me to...
and keeping your heart safe... always.
I'll keep the faith for you, when you simply can't.

And there it is, time and time again,

That "gray place" to which he vanishes in thought.

He sits so still… he ponders…

Challenges large and small,

People kind and mean,

Events now and then.

Soon he "returns" and lights up.

Gray is gone.

Wonderful Winnipesaukee Memories

Lake Winnipesaukee sunset

Warm sunshine brushes my face
The dancing breeze toys with my hair
His infectious laughter intoxicates my senses
He extends his arm – I lovingly wrap around him.
We walk together – laughing, loving, living
In our own world – private, poignant, passionate
Filled with our love – plentiful, powerful, perfect.

Warm expressions of love soothe my heart
The dancing words toy with my desire
His energy intoxicates my soul
He opens his heart – I willingly wrap his love
around me.

Celebrating 10th wedding anniversary on cruise ship

Happy New Year

Twilight in Newport, Rhode Island

Passing through the
Panama Canal

Ron making time with three babes in Montreal, Canada, 2012

Cathy & Ron on the deck at Martingale Wharf in Portsmouth, New Hampshire

Then I see
his gaze upon me;
I am captured –
I am whole.

My heart melts –
wide windows open
now revealing
one shared soul.

Within his eyes
a "just believe" answer
lifts my spirits
and lets me soar.

Day by day
he wants me to love him,
which I shall
forever more.

View from the Sunset Grille
at the Grove Park Inn,
Asheville, North Carolina

Now, wherever I am
      I am filled with
           thoughts of you.

And I get such a rush my flesh jumps!

With a knowing smile,
      I just pause,
           close my eyes,

And I feel my skin flush with goose bumps!

Along came challenges…
   Long ago, I gave up on dreams,
   Fairy tales,
      And happily ever afters.

I closed all windows to my soul
   And shifted into a
     Busy, so-called
       Worthwhile existence.

Along came you...
  Looking into your eyes
    I saw
      The sparkle of Life.

I heard your words
  And recognized
    Elusive
      Truth.

Along came awakening...
   Walls didn't crumble –
    They
             Disintegrated.

Ice didn't
  melt –
   It
          Exploded.

Along came Life...
   The splendor of actually
     Feeling myself living
       Blossomed.

My heart is touched
  And my
    Soul
      Rekindled.

Manchester Mill Yard sunset
New Hampshire

Beauty in our back yard

The celebrations continue!

North pasture view at Silver Fox Farm, Mill Spring, North Carolina

Golden sunset in Appalachian Mountains in North Carolina

Harbor in St. Barth's

**Left: Ron signals for drink service in St. Lucia
Right: at the Brimstone Hill Fortress in St. Kitts**

On board ship in Guadaloupe

"Just another day...
for you and me in Paradise."

Our adventures continue...

Mt. Vesuvius & Pompeii
ruins, Italy

Visiting St. Martin / St. Maarten

We snorkeled here in St. John

Loving the Italian Alps at the Grand Tremezzo, Lake Como, Italy

The Ronald checking real estate in St. Moritz, Switzerland

Lake Garda, Italy's largest lake, between Venice and Milan

I appreciate how fully you love me.
You lift me when I'm down,
and celebrate with me when I'm up.
You direct me when I'm scattered,
and even listen when I *think* I'm profound.
You treat me with full respect as a person,
and demonstrate all the chivalry
that the finest knight would grant his
ladylove.

Ron near Rialto Bridge in Venice, Italy

View from Rialto Bridge, Venice, Italy

Ron strolling a street in Split, Croatia

Ron in Rome;
"Can you hear me now?"

Ron inspecting news stand
in Portofino, Italy

Visiting the Colosseum in Rome, Italy

El Ronaldo holding up the Leaning Tower of Pisa in Italy

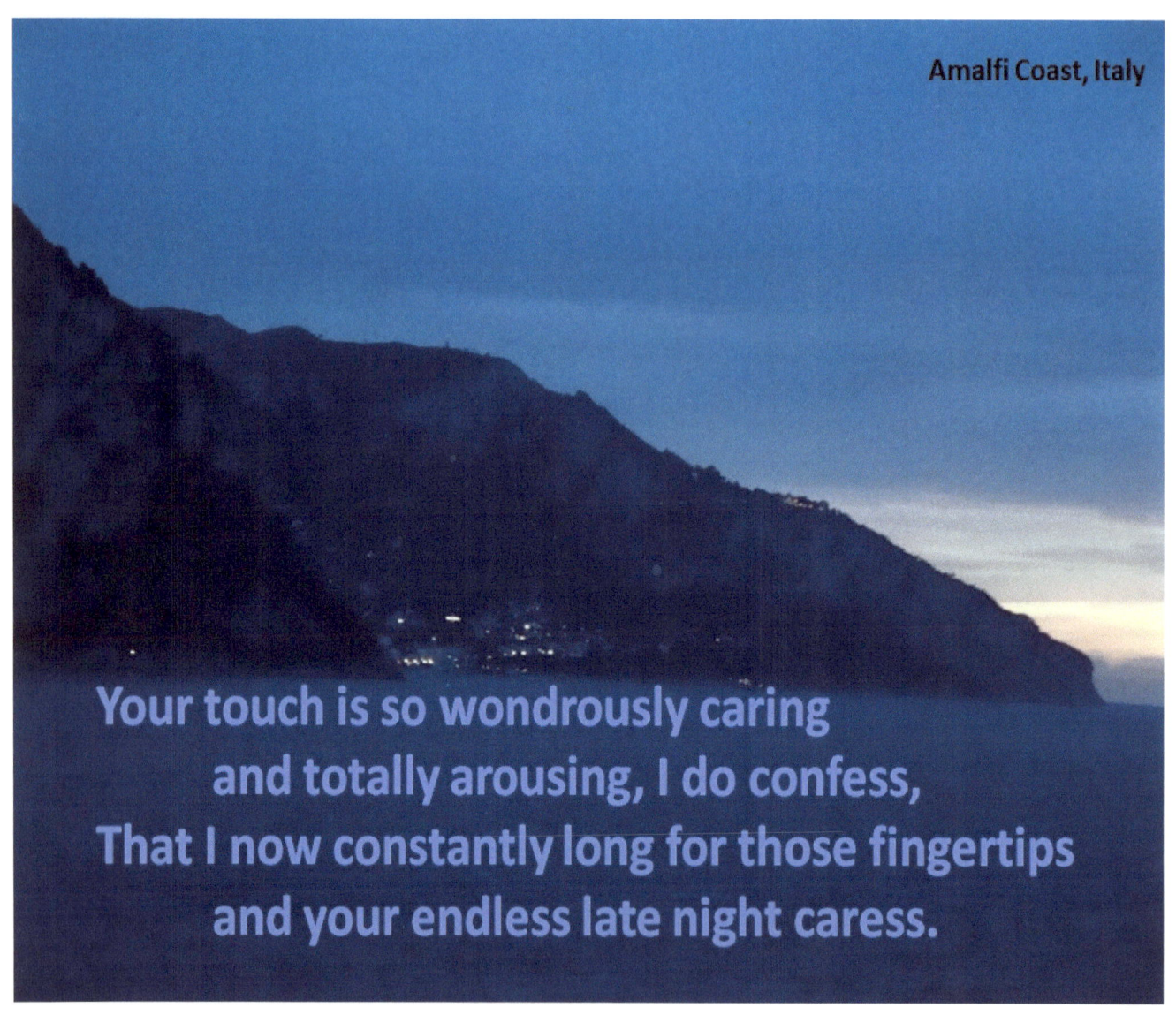

Amalfi Coast, Italy

Your touch is so wondrously caring
and totally arousing, I do confess,
That I now constantly long for those fingertips
and your endless late night caress.

Ron tossing 3 coins in the Trevi Fountain, Rome, Italy

Entering picture-perfect Portofino, Italy

Visiting The Biltmore,
Asheville, North Carolina

In this adventure of our life together,
I love showing you how wonderful you are to love.

Left to Right: Keira, Ron, Nina, Chris, Adam & Cathy

"Together" also meant plenty of
family adventures for this happily
self-proclaimed Evil Stepmother, too!

Oia on Santorini

Cathy in Fira, Santorini, our favorite Greek island

Ron in Monaco, overlooking yachts in the harbor

Lufthansa First Class...
Ron says, "What do you mean I have trouble relaxing?"

Tuscany countryside in Italy

Ron exploring old fort in Barcelona, Spain

We are happily where we belong... together... wherever that may be and wherever that may lead us.

Swimming with the stingrays at Georgetown, Grand Cayman

Playing with
Sea Wolves in Uruguay

White water rafting on Costa Rica's Rio Pacuare, site of 2011 World Rafting Championship

One of Ron's most endearing charms... a superb sense of humor.

What do you mean Ron has a wide yawn? <u>THIS</u> is a wide yawn!

Ron & Jim Powers hamming at
Billy's Sports Bar
& Ron celebrating
St. Patrick's Day at 900°
Both in Manchester, NH

"Blessed are the cracked, for they let in the light!"

Ed Davis & Ron being "boys" during a cruise

Ron and Dr. J
shopping in
Nazareth, Israel

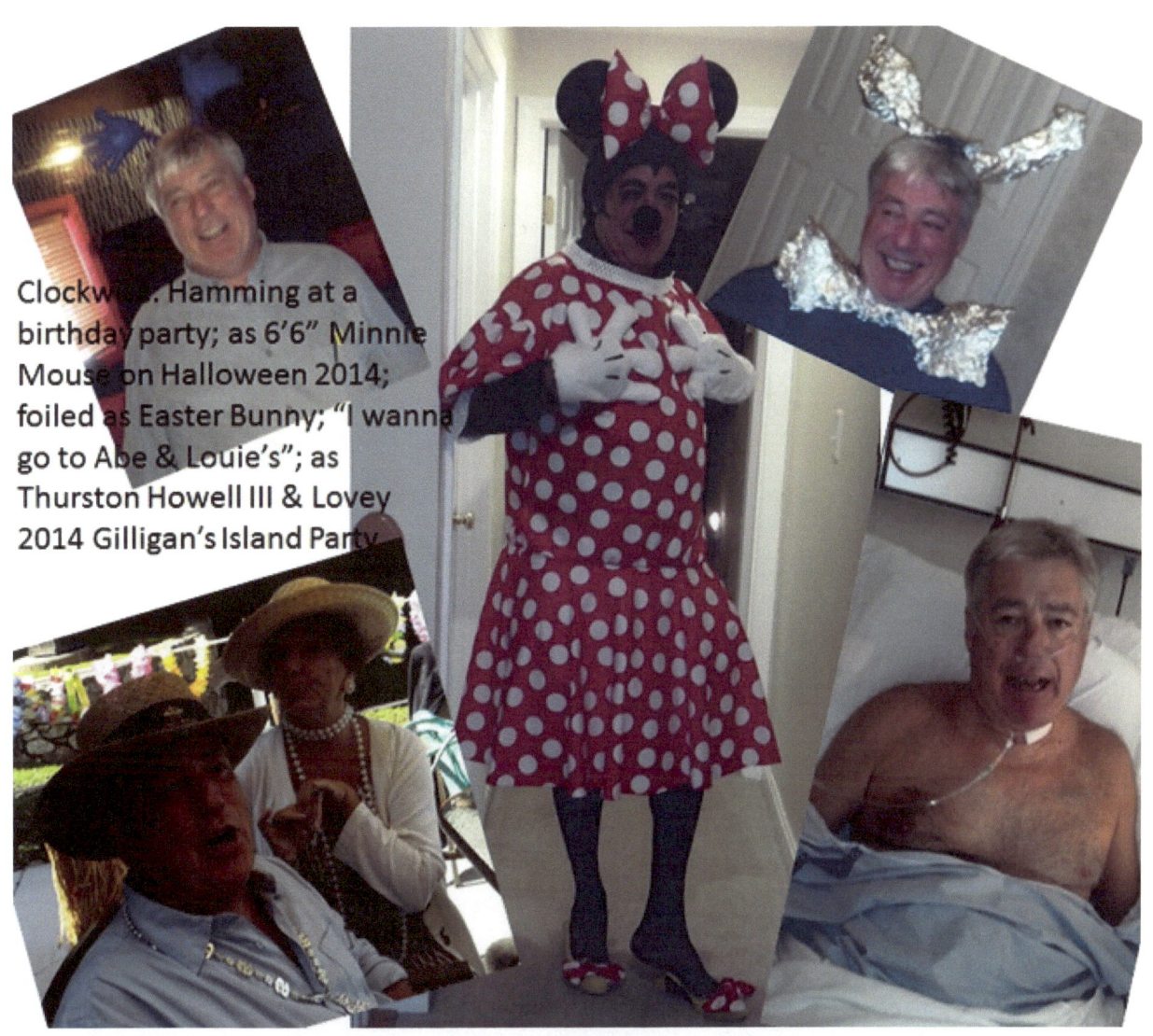

Clockwise: Hamming at a birthday party; as 6'6" Minnie Mouse on Halloween 2014; foiled as Easter Bunny; "I wanna go to Abe & Louie's"; as Thurston Howell III & Lovey 2014 Gilligan's Island Party

His sense of humor is legendary!

Which one of you gents is *really* "the most interesting man in the world???"

No question, Babe. It's YOU!

Ron hamming with artist
Graham Denison
on Mediterranean Celebrity cruise

With each passing year,
my Darling,
I remain a steadfast
keeper of all that is
precious inside of you...
your heart and soul,
your faith <u>and</u> frailties,
your love and trust.

My heart has never been as full of love,
nor my soul
so full of hope.

My prayer; my deepest desire
is to make you feel happy
and secure and trusted and
loved... completely.

And I will go to the ends of the earth
to make your dreams come true....
I love you.